(The PUncS)

An introduction to the story of punctuation

Barbara Cooper

illustrated by Maggie Raynor

COMPASS

Meet the Puncs

Did you know that 'Puncs' are punctuation marks? (If you thought that they were <u>punks</u>, you were wrong.)

You cannot escape from them: they are everywhere.

Without them there would be a dreadful muddle. There wouldn't be any sentences; there would only be words going on

for ever...

and ever...

and ever...

Without sentences there would be no point in anybody trying to write stories, or letters, or messages — or anything else worth reading.

So it is no good being clever—clever and thinking to yourself:

"I don't care about the Puncs."

You'd be much happier if you found out all about them!

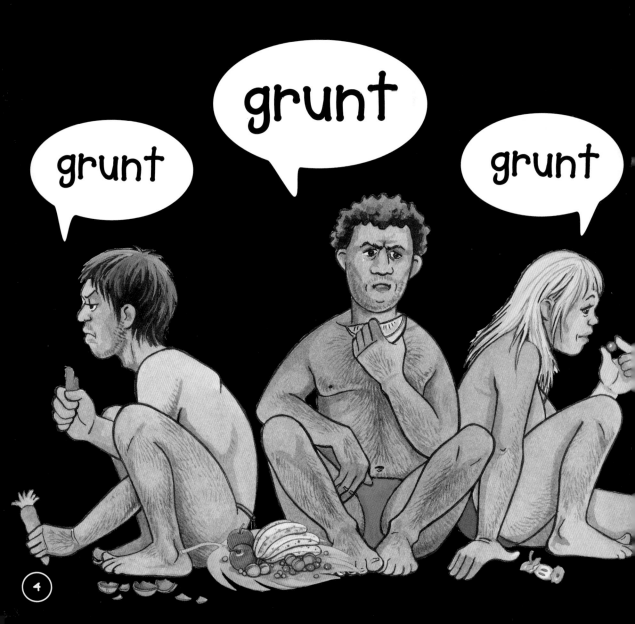

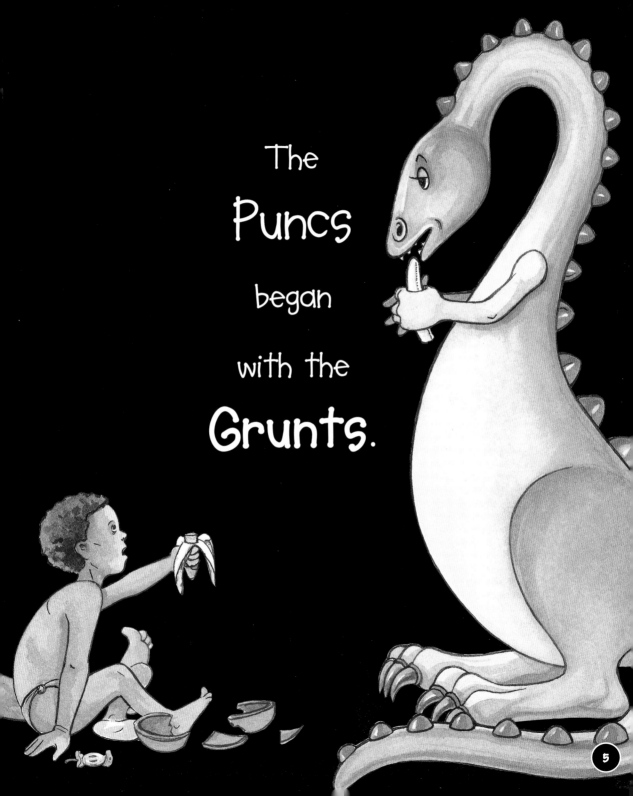

The
Puncs
began
with the
Grunts.

Many thousands of years ago
(nobody really knows when)

the Grunts

became

Words.

The

Words

became

Pictures.

The

Pictures

became

Letters.

The Letters became Writing.

At first it didn't
look like Writing.

It looked like this.

And this.

And this.

Then, gradually, all over the world, people learned how to turn the sounds of their many different languages (which had begun with the Grunts) into many different kinds of Writing.

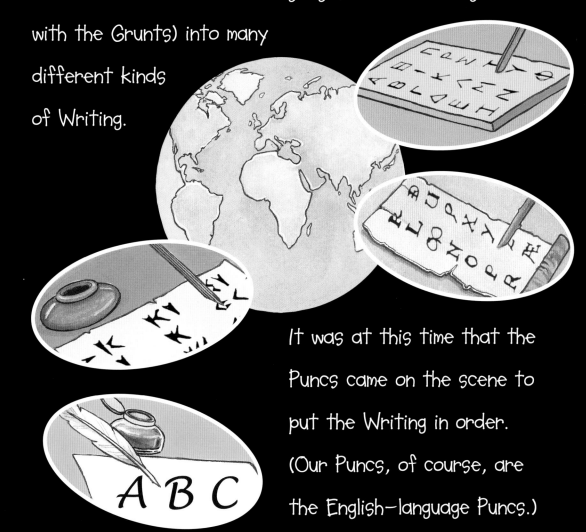

It was at this time that the Puncs came on the scene to put the Writing in order. (Our Puncs, of course, are the English-language Puncs.)

First came the Early Puncs.

Out in front were armies of fearless Full Stops.

Followed by companies of Colons.

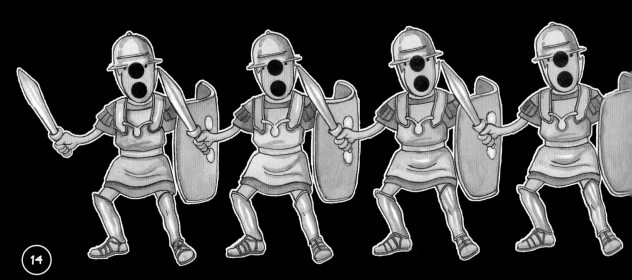

Several hundred years later, the Middle Puncs appeared. First came columns of Commas and Question Marks.

Followed by squadrons of Semi-Colons.

And hordes of Hyphens.

Scribes, whose job it was to copy books, took a whole week to finish one page – and as hardly anyone could read, only a few people knew about the Puncs.

Then someone had the idea of making a machine which could print thousands of words in a day. The Early and Middle Puncs became frantically busy.
(But the Scribes were no longer needed.)

For another few hundred years there was little change, until the arrival of the Later Puncs. First came battalions of Brackets,

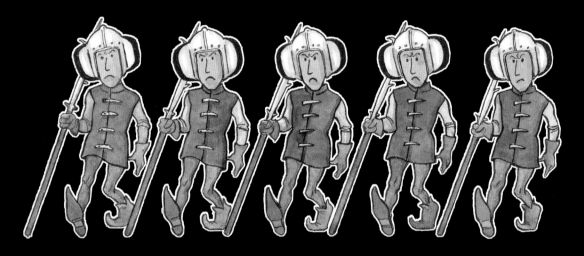

followed by regiments of eager Exclamation Marks,

armies of Apostrophes,

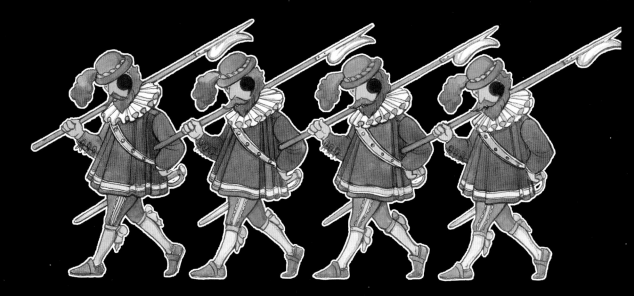

and divisions of Dashes.

In the year 1620, some of the Puncs sailed across

the Atlantic Ocean in a ship called the 'Mayflower'.

They were known as the **'Pilgrim Puncs'**.

The pilgrims landed at a place which they named

'Punc Rock'. (Not to be confused with

Punk Rock!)

Just when it looked as though the Puncs and the Writing had settled down happily among the Sentences there was an unexpected invasion of Speech Marks.

First came the Double Speech Marks.

Followed by their close relations, the
Single Speech Marks.

Finally, at last, and right at the end, came lines
of **Ellipses**, marching three-by-three...

Wherever they were – north, south, east or west – the Puncs had to fight hard.

north

east

south

west

Their struggles were known as the

'Wars of the Words'.

After winning several fierce battles, the Puncs finally settled down peacefully among their chosen languages.

以標點 潤飾拗口言語

在聯合標點組織及世界言語協會進行的一次會議，協定標點和言語之間不再有抵觸。以下是發表的聲明：

「在每一個家和每一種語言，我們將會協力達到使所有作品讀起來有趣的目的。」

أوقات بانك

يضفي البانك سلاما على عالم الكلمات المتحاربة

في احدى اجتماعات الـديو بـي او (منظمـة بانـك المتحدة) و الـ دابليو دابليـو ايـة (رابطـة الكلمات العالمية) تـم الموافقـة علـى انه لـن يكـون هنـاك حرب بيـن بانك و الكلمـات. و اصدر البيان التالي:

"فـي جميـع البـلاد و اللغات سنوحد اهدافنا مـن اجل جعل جميـع انـواع الكتابـة مقروءة."

PUNCS BRING PEACE TO WORLD OF WARRING WORD

At a meeting of the UPO (United Puncs Organisation) and t WWA (Worldwide Words Associatio it was agreed that there will be no

Here are some other Puncs from around the World

Alfonso Apostrofo '	Spanish
Nader Naghlé Ghowl :	Farsi
Vincenzo Virgola ,	Italian
Daisuke Dasshu –	Japanese
Essa Ela Akherehi …	Arabic
Nellie Neuggim Pyo !	Korean
Tomaso Tochka .	Russian
Samir Sawalia Nishann –	Urdu
Nazime Noktali Virgul ;	Turkish
Ayo Ami Ibere ?	Yoruba
Alfreda Aufrungszeichen ' '	German
Gerard and Ghislaine Guillemet " "	French
Kim Kuohao ( )	Chinese

...ore wars between the Puncs ...d the Words. The following ...atement was issued:

..."In every country and ...ery language, we will ...e united in our aim to ...make all kinds of ...writing readable."

Today, our Puncs are busier than ever.
It's time you met them all...

Fergus Full Stop
P.C. (Punc Constable) Full
Stop thinks of himself as No. 1
(Number One) Punc. He is a
traffic cop. He can bring cars
and lorries and buses and
bicycles and vans to a .

Ethel Exclamation Mark
is the tallest and the thinnest
of the Puncs! She is a head
teacher and knows exactly how
to make children behave
themselves!
No-one dares disobey her!

Quentin
Quentin Question Mark
Have you heard of this Punc**?** Did you know that he is a Customs Officer**?** Do you know where he works**?**

Alec Apostrophe is the skipper of a fishin**'** boat called the *Jolly Punc*. Alec**'**s life is very busy. He**'**s always in a hurry and speaks extremely quickly, shortenin**'** words (don**'**t, can**'**t, won**'**t) and droppin**'** **'**is (his) h**'**s and g**'**s.

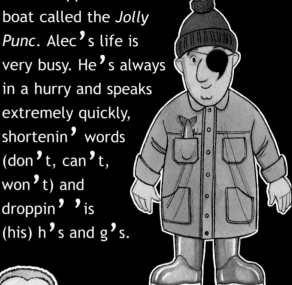

Colin Comma**,** the singing postman**,** is the healthiest**,** happiest**,** and most cheerful Punc. He works very hard**,** as a postman in the morning**,** as a window cleaner in the afternoon**,** and as a van-driver at night**,** etc.**,** etc.**,** etc.

Henrietta
Henrietta Hyphen-Hyphen of Hyphen-on-the-Hill is a very well-connected Punc. She often hob-nobs with Royalty.

A.P. (Able Punc) **Barrington** Brackets

is all ears (as you can see from his picture). His head is full of (secret military) facts. His ship is an aircraft carrier (called the *Punc Royal*).

Ellie Ellipsis

is the oldest and the wisest Punc... or so she says. She is an astrologer... and she tells people's fortunes. She drops off to sleep, so her sentences always end like this...

Danny Dash

is a famous footballing Punc. He plays for Punc United — dashing about from one end of the pitch to the other — passing and tackling and heading — and — now and again — scoring goals.

PCS (Punc Colour Sergeant) **Charlie** Colon

is a military Punc: a true leader. He leads one lot of words into another: like this.

Selina Semi-Colon

is a tour guide; has been doing the same job for many years; has always worked for Punc Express Tours; speaks several languages.

Samita and Sachin Speech Marks

are identical twins. One starts a sentence and the other finishes it.
"We can't bear" says Samita,
"to be apart," says Sachin.

Now that you have been introduced to

(**P**The**u**n**cS**)

you can see how very useful
and important they are.

However, they are in serious danger,
because some people just
don't care about them any more.

You can be a good friend to the Puncs
by never forgetting them,
never leaving them out, and always
putting them in the right place.